BERLIN: CITY AND HISTORY

So this is the New Berlin – Berlin on the threshold between the second and the third millenniums. Now that all the millennium rockets have burned out, all the champagne corks have been recycled and all the anthems have been sung, we are left with a Berlin that offers more of everything: bigger, better, brighter, faster, funnier, higher, richer, more expensive, more fascinating, more powerful, more intelligent, more glittering and more amoral and immoral than all the other major cities surrounding it.

Three capitals dominated the Old World: London, Paris and Berlin. Superlatives should always be consumed with caution, of course – their expiry date is undefined. Pride goes before a fall, and an injudicious lust for status can have disagreeable consequences. The Berliners themselves, natives even though most of them were not actually born within the city limits, are generally characterised by common sense and healthy scepticism. Their basic attitude is best expressed by their untranslatable "Uns kann keener." Literally this means, "Nobody can us." Precisely what nobody can is left open to the imagination, however, and this is a key element of the Berliners' character. Among other things, the saying expresses their underdeveloped fear of authority and

their lack of respect for things new and different.

The basic story of the city's development is sketched in the Chronology on pages 6 and 7. One thing that is striking in Berlin's history is that the impetus for change always came from outside. On reflection, however, this is not really so surprising. Berlin lay on the lifeline between the Amber Coast on the Baltic Sea and the depths of the Ukraine, and also on the trade route between the salt mines in the south and icy Novgorod in the north. And the region around the city had little in the way of its own resources: just rye and oak wood. Bronze and iron tools and utensils had to be imported from the Erzgebirge Mountains. Furs and hides came from Russia, cloth from Flanders. Other wares recorded in historical bills of lading include silk, saffron, ginger, pepper, wine and herrings. For a while the monasteries monopolised the trade in salt, beer and lime, but eventually their power waned and the abbots were driven out of the city. In addition to their other traits, the Berliners were also never particularly God-fearing.

Other settlements in the German-speaking territories were originally much more important and influential: Cologne, Augsburg, Nuremberg, Trier, Lübeck, Lüneburg, Magdeburg, Stralsund. The people here have never really been all that afraid of embracing change and new arrivals. The story of Count Friedrich IV of Nuremberg is a typical example. On 30 April 1415, at the Council of Constance, Emperor Sigismund granted Friedrich the Mark of Brandenburg by lien. The worthy Friedrich immediately started referring to himself as "Elector of the Holy Roman Empire and Margrave of Brandenburg". His prospective subjects were duly impressed by this title, which sounds even more pompous in German, and on 18 October of the same year the worthies of the city council pressed a "Deed of Probity" into Friedrich's aristocratic hand. This was typical – instead of starting a bloody conflict they simply worked out a practical arrangement. Everyone who came was integrated, and they all came: the pious believers from the Rhine, the Jews from Austria, the Bohemians and the Huguenots. Live and let live was the people's watchword. Or, in the words of Friedrich the Great, "Everyone should be free to find happiness in their own fashion."

Four dates dominate the more recent history of the German capital: 1871, when Berlin was made capital of the German Empire; 1945, when the capital of the Nazi Reich was taken by the troops of the Red Army; 1961 when the infamous Berlin Wall was built in a single August night; and 1989 when the Wall that had separated East and West Berlin for 28 years finally fell.

The Berlin of the year 2000, this modern city with its millions of inhabitants, is both new and a logical historical outcome of the events of 1871, 1945, 1961 and 1989. Initially, the prospect of Berlin once again being Germany's capital caused some concern in the cabinets of Europe's other nations. For a while there was even some alarmist talk of a new and possibly threatening "Berlin Republic". Bonn was familiar, it was associated with the cosily small-scale, with the good cheer of the Rhineland and traditional German virtues like uprightness, shops that closed punctually at six thirty and a ban on the use of car horns after ten. And Berlin?

Would Berlin really be nothing but dross, trumpery, haste, superficiality and a new gold rush with all the negative consequences that those things entail, as the doomsayers claimed?

None of the dire predictions came true. The German Government and Parliament's move to Berlin was smooth and uneventful. The necessary reorganisation went without a hitch, there was no gold rush or anything like it and the rents fell instead of rising. The politicians didn't get stranded in the provinces on their way to work and the civil servants didn't all fly home at the taxpayers' expense every Thursday. Instead, they sensibly brought their families to Berlin, initially for the occasional weekend and then for good. The building costs for the new ministries rose, but within reason. Rulers and the ruled alike have come to terms with the everyday reality of their respective power and powerlessness, and everyone goes about their own characteristic activities: The scientists furrow their brows, the jet-set kiss exaltedly at their glittering parties, the detractors take offence, the optimists rejoice, the gourmet chefs labour over their pots, the star tenors hit the high C, the pessimists plumb the depths of despair, the vamps and urban amazons coo and flutter their eyelids. The workaday dream-

Reichstag with glass cupola ▽

DEM DEUTSCHEN VOLKE

ers build their visions and when darkness falls the night-owls spread out in search of amusement.

Mediocrity? Run of the mill? Au contraire. Here we find theatre directors who enjoy the most damning reviews as though they were effulgent praise. Orchestras led by star conductors who turn every elegant stroke of their illustrious batons to pure gold. Galleries where the spin doctors of the art scene dictate prices in seven-digit figures. Mammon and the Muses are joined at the hip. Those who still try to separate art and commerce are either too good or too naïve for this world of show business. The globalised trade in works of genius is not to be had for a song – unless it's a song that goes triple platinum in the first week.

Municipal politics are a major league affair in the Berlin of the 2000 era. Forget about soup kitchens, subsidised day care centre fees and correctly standardised children's playgrounds. Municipal officials juggle with works by Rubens and Picasso, with arts budgets running into the billions, with thirty theatres and a veritable cornucopia of renowned artists and performers. Park benches in the pedestrian zones are irrelevant.

That's simply the way it is; part of it is the arrogance generated by sheer scale. Nobody really poses

▽ The Potsdamer Platz with Sony Center

any serious questions about latent conflicts between the city and the surrounding region. Mere details, irrelevant. Four million people now live in Greater Berlin. To understand the European dimension one only needs to remember how close Potsdam is to Frankfurt on the Oder in former East Germany, and also to Prague, Poland and the Czech Republic. This city is a hub for people, ideas, capital and services, and this creates both opportunities and responsibilities. A century ago, when the railway started to shape the old imperial city of Berlin, it transformed the often helpless old city from a stodgy and conservative royal capital into a gigantic Moloch of the industrial revolution. In 1900 Berlin was like a huge transit station.

Today, in the Berlin of the third millennium, in the centre of the European Union with a single currency and no borders, the age of factory soot and bourgeois conservatism is over. What count now are alertness and tolerance, boldness and careful planning, the willingness to take risks and unswerving perseverance. In short, it is a world of contradictions, and the Berliners have to handle it on their own.

This eternal conflict between yesterday and today, between the loud and the quiet, above and below, good and bad: this is Berlin!

Chronology of the History of Berlin

Circa 50000 BC

Earliest known human settlement in what is now the district of Neukölln in the south of Berlin, determined by the discovery of bone fragments in a gravel pit.

Circa 9000 BC

Settlement of reindeer hunters on the Tegeler Fliess in the north of Berlin.

Circa 3000 BC

Finds of funnel beaker culture pottery in Berlin-Britz show that people lived here in a certain degree of comfort.

946 AD

Establishment of the Bishopric of Havelberg.

948

Establishment of the Bishopric of Brandenburg.

1134

The Ascanian leader AlbrechtI the Bear takes over and subjugates the region after being instated as margrave by Emperor Lothar III.

1180

Foundation of Lehnin Abbey. The abbots send monks out into the surrounding country to drain the marshes and cultivate the fields along the River Spree – in the area where the Reichstag, Chancellery, Brandenburg Gate, Unter den Linden boulevard and the Friedrichstrasse are now located.

28 October 1237

First documented mention of "Cölln" on the River Spree.

1244

First documented mention of the name "Berlin". The name probably originates from Albrecht I, known as "The Bear". It is unlikely that this referred to bear-like strength, however, but rather to Albrecht's home town of Bernburg in the Harz Mountains.

1251

Berlin is granted exemption from customs duties and experiences its first economic flowering. Fabrics from Flanders are traded, as are dried cod and herrings from the sea ports. Berlin beer has an excellent reputation and is exported to Hamburg and Lübeck. Rich citizens drink wines from Spain, Greece and Italy. Local wine is grown in Berlin, on the Oder river and in the region around Guben and Cottbus.

1261

First documented mention of the margravial court as the seat of government in Berlin (aula berlin). It was located in what is now the Klosterstrasse in Berlin Mitte.

1272

The Bakers' League drafts its first deed of incorporation, laying the foundation of the craftsmen's guilds, whose charters precisely regulated members' rights, laws, obligations and moral principles. This led to an early form of medieval grass-roots democracy, in which the master craftsmen became one of the mainstays of the non-aristocratic patricians. In contrast to the world of hereditary nobility, the guilds enabled people, even those from the lowest classes, to rise to higher stations by means of talent, hard work and honesty.

1280

First appearance of a heraldic design with two bears facing one another in the coat of arms of the furriers' guild. The animal on the official city seal is still the eagle, however. The bear (walking on all fours) was not adopted as the symbol of the city authorities until 1338. It has remained Berlin's proud heraldic mascot down to the present day.

1285

First use of coffins made of wood for the burial of rich men. Women and the poor are still buried in sacks.

1294

First mention of the Church of Our Lady (Marienkirche).

1307

The members of the Four Guilds – bakers, cobblers, butchers and clothiers – form an "unio", officially uniting the settlements of Berlin and Cölln. The two halves of the city are connected by a primitive bridge, the Mühlendamm.

1411

Emperor Sigismund instates Count Friedrich VI of Nuremberg, from the Franconian lineage of the House of Hohenzollern, as hereditary governor. Thenceforth, the Hohenzollerns rule Brandenburg, later Prussia and the German Empire. Their dominion doesn't end until the abdication of Kaiser Wilhelm II in 1918, who then leaves Berlin forever.

1538

The New Mark of Brandenburg becomes Lutheran.

1539

The Old Mark also converts to Lutherism.

1640

Friedrich Wilhelm, known respectfully as the Great Elector (Grosser Kurfürst) since the battle of Fehrbellin, takes the helm of a state ravaged by the Thirty Years' War. The population has fallen to less than 6,000.

16 April 1647

Elector Friedrich Wilhelm orders the planting of a line of lindens and walnut trees from the New Bridge to Brandenburg Gate, creating the road that is to become Berlin's lifeline and fashionable boulevard: Unter den Linden (Beneath the Lindens).

8 November 1685

In the Edict of Potsdam Prussia officially invites the persecuted French Calvinist Huguenots to settle in the city, a decision that is to have far-reaching consequences for Berlin's history and the politics of Prussia. Leading traders, craftsmen, scholars and artists settle in the city and the population grows to nearly 30,000.

18 January 1701
Elector Friedrich III, who has ruled since 1688, is crowned King Friedrich I of Prussia in his home city of Königsberg.

1704
The Vossische Zeitung appears for the first time. It is the very first newspaper that is also read outside the borders of the city. Censorship is still a matter of course but it is handled quite liberally.

1713
The "Soldier King" Friedrich Wilhelm I ascends the throne and begins an unprecedented reformation and expansion of the armed forces. The French envoy states presciently, "Other states have an army. Prussia is an army that has a state."

1721
The first coffee shop opens in the Lustgarten. A "nectarial coffee beverage" is served in paper-thin cups made of Chinese porcelain.

1737
Nearly a thousand new houses have been built along Unter den Linden boulevard since 1721.

1740
Friedrich II ascends the throne and implements many reforms. He permits a lottery, the first in Berlin, with 20,000 tickets for 5 talers each, and repeals the censorship of the press.

7 December 1742
Opening of the Royal Opera House on Unter den Linden with a performance of Graun's Caesar and Cleopatra.

1744
Commencement of the construction of Schloss Sanssouci.

1764
Giacomo Casanova visits Berlin and stays at the Drei Lilien. In his memoirs the Venetian beau refers to the simple inn grandly as the "Hôtel du Paris".

1778
Johann Wolfgang von Goethe visits Berlin and stays at the city's finest establishment, Gasthaus zur Sonne on Unter den Linden boulevard.

1789
Wolfgang Amadeus Mozart visits Berlin and stays at the Schwarzer Adler. Mozart politely refuses the position of Prussian Orchestra Director offered to him by Friedrich Wilhelm II.

6 August 1791
Brandenburg Gate is opened to the general public. The Quadriga statue with the four horses is added in 1796. Total construction costs: 111,000 talers.

1804
Friedrich Schiller visits Berlin and stays at the Hôtel de Russie. It is the same inn on Unter den Linden where Goethe stayed, with a new name.

1848
Revolution in Berlin. King Friedrich Wilhelm IV is in serious danger of deposition. His brother Wilhelm flees the city but later becomes regent (26 October 1858) when his brother is incapacitated by a stroke. Wilhelm is crowned king on 2 January 1861 and then kaiser (in Versailles) on 18 January 1871.

1888
The year of the three kaisers: After the death of old Wilhelm I his terminally ill son Friedrich III assumes "power" for 99 days, but his tracheal cancer is too advanced to allow him to leave any real mark on the affairs of the state. Bismarck administers the

empire, deeply concerned that Britain's influence is growing too strong. Friedrich's wife, Empress "Vicky" (daughter of Queen Victoria) is a constant thorn in the side of both the Iron Chancellor and her own son, Wilhelm II.. Wilhelm turns Prussia and Germany into a nation at arms.

1914
Start of World War I.

1918
Abdication of the last German Kaiser.

1920
The formation of Greater Berlin, population: 3.8 million.

1933
Hitler takes power. The Reichstag burns down on February 27. and 28. Book burning on the Opernplatz.

1936
The Olympic Games in Berlin.

1939
Beginning of World War II.

1943
First major air raids on Berlin.

1945
Hitler's suicide and capitulation of the Wehrmacht. The city is divided into four zones and made headquarters of the Allied Council.

1948/1949
Land blockade of West Berlin by the Soviets. Supplies for the city's two million people are maintained with a massive airlift.

1961
Construction of the Berlin Wall.

1989
Opening of the Berlin Wall.

1990
Reunification of Germany.

1999
The German Government officially convenes for its first session in Berlin.

2001
Rezoning reduces the former 23 city districts to twelve.

KURFÜRSTENDAMM BOULEVARD
Charlottenburg-Wilmersdorf

A hundred years ago an elegant business and residential district grew up outside the traditional city centre: the Neue Westen (New West) along Kurfürstendamm boulevard, which had originated in 1550 as a path in the former hunting grounds. Bismarck made the first plans in 1875 and 25 years later the Deutsche Bank financed the property that fuelled the gold rush. Progress was fast and lasting. Luxurious houses, restaurants, offices, medical practices, pastry shops, night clubs, theatres and art galleries attracted the rich and nouveau-riche alike. Cinemas were also a prominent feature: The Marmorhaus, opened in 1912, is the oldest surviving example, but the Astor is also famous. After the blockade and the building of the Wall the "Ku'damm" became the centre of the western sector. Despite predictions to the contrary, it has lost none of its splendour, with famous fashion houses and top designers adding to the attractions. The famous **Hotel Kempinski** and **Café Kranzler** are also still in the same places, the latter now renovated with a new look.

▽ *The "Berlin" Sculpture*

THE "BERLIN" SCULPTURE

Charlottenburg-Wilmersdorf, Tauentziensstrasse

Martin Matschinsky and his wife Brigitte Denninghoff were two of the European artists commissioned in 1987 to create a sculpture symbolising Berlin at the end of the 20th century. Their joint work Berlin was one of the most widely regarded, clearly expressing the divides still experienced within the new unity. The sculpture has lost none of its relevance today.

CITY CENTRE

Charlottenburg-Wilmersdorf
Kurfürstendamm, Tauentziensstrasse

Zoo Station · KaDeWe · Europa Center

Tauentziensstrasse between Wittenbergplatz and the Kaiser Wilhelm Memorial Church has been a busy bazaar ever since the 20s, partly because of the proximity of the central **Zoo Railway Station**. The great shopping temples, colourfully illuminated until late at night, attract both trendy youngsters and older, well-to-do conservatives with a penchant for elegance. A stroll on Tauentziensstrasse is not complete

▽ *Kurfürstendamm boulevard, Kranzler corner*

Kurfürstendamm boulevard ▽

Zoo railway station ▽

without an extended visit to **KaDeWe**, Europe's biggest department store. At the other end of the stylish street the renovated **Europa Center** now stands on the site of the former Romanisches Café, which was once frequented by avant-garde writers like Brecht and Kästner. Albert Einstein read his morning papers here, and the chain-smoking chess grand master Emanuel Lasker spent hours here playing for money in the company of renowned painters like the young, indigent Oskar Kokoschka. The foreign minister and later chancellor Gustav Stresemann also lived nearby, within sight of

Breitscheidplatz and next door to Emil Nolde. Their homes were destroyed by the air raids in the winter of 1944–45. Today, the classical Wilhelminian mansions have been replaced by a skyline of towering postmodernist office blocks that form the commercial centre of the new district of Charlottenburg-Wilmersdorf. The finest piece of new architecture here is the glittering glass building at the intersection with Joachimstaler Strasse designed by star architect Helmut Jahn.

▽ *Europa Center*

△ Tiffany's terrace café   ▽ Breitscheidplatz, Globe Fountain (Weltkugelbrunnen, 1983)   △ Water clock

KAISER WILHELM MEMORIAL CHURCH
Charlottenburg-Wilmersdorf, Breitscheidplatz

The Kaiser-Wilhelm-Gedächtniskirche was built between 1891 and 1895 to commemorate the first Hohenzollern emperor of Germany. Designed by Franz Schwechten in the late Romanesque style of the Rhineland, it had a 113-metre spire. Theologian Albert Schweitzer made his debut as an organist in the church in 1899. Bomb damage in World War II was so severe that the Berlin Senate decided to demolish the building in 1956. This was prevented by storm of popular protest throughout Berlin, and professor of architecture Egon Eiermann from Karlsruhe conceived a bold reconstruction combining old and new elements that was completed in 1963. Colloquially, the new structure is referred to as the "lipstick and powder compact", not without respect. Both the deep blue glass bricks of the new church and the priceless mosaics (unique allegories of the lives of the German emperors) in the base of the original bell tower were recently restored to their original harmonious beauty. Recommended: Sunday organ vespers.

▽ *Kaiser Wilhelm Memorial Church, altar and cross*   *Kaiser Wilhelm Memorial Church* ▷

SCHLOSS CHARLOTTENBURG
Charlottenburg-Wilmersdorf
Spandauer Damm, Luisenplatz

(Charlottenburg Palace) The controversial debate over the rebuilding of the old Berliner Stadtschloss (City Palace) in the Lustgarten also made the second palace complex in central Berlin a focus of discussion. It was completed under the aegis of Friedrich the Great and is one of the longest buildings in Germany (505.5m). A terrible air raid on 23 November 1943 left it little more than an empty shell, but it was rebuilt in the 1950s – a project facilitated greatly by the fact that much of the original furnishings had been removed in the 19th century and could be recovered. The palace is still historically significant, despite its almost complete reconstruction. The first architect Johann A. Nehring was commissioned to build a pleasant summer residence for Sophie Charlotte, the wife of Elector Friedrich III, on the site in the village of Lietzow. However, when the Hohenzollern prince became King of Prussia in 1701 he decided to turn it into a much more extensive and elegant palace. The Swedish architect Eosander von Göthe added

▽ *Schloss Charlottenburg (Charlottenburg Palace)*

the domed tower, the great orangery and the court wing, but the finishing touches were the work of Georg W. von Knobelsdorff, who was also responsible for the magnificent new rooms in the east wing. Friedrich the Great spent very little time in the City Palace, alternating instead between Charlottenburg and Sanssouci. After his death his nephew Friedrich Wilhelm II commissioned Carl Gotthard Langhans to build the Kleines Schlosstheater. Langhans also designed the Belvedere tea house in the Schlosspark. Today it houses an outstanding collection of Berlin porcelain, including early works by Wilhelm Caspar Wegely, the almost forgotten industrialist and pioneer of Prussian porcelain-making (1751). An even finer and historically more important collection can be seen in the Porzellan-Kabinett in the Schloss, with classic 17th-century blue and white porcelain from China. After severe damage in the War many unique pieces were sold at auctions.

Porcelain museum (Porzellan-Kabinett) ▽

STRASSE DES 17. JUNI · VICTORY COLUMN
Mitte, Strasse des 17. Juni, Grosser Stern

Originally, the 3km long June 17th Street was a narrow riding path running through the electors' **Tiergarten park**. It grew gradually in size and importance, and at the end of the 30s Hitler's architect Albert Speer turned it into a triumphal boulevard for the masters of the New Reich, complete with striking candelabra lamps. Fewer than 700 of the over 200,000 trees in the Tiergarten survived the War and the Berlin Blockade, but donations from all over Germany enabled a major reforestation

◁ *Victory Column*

project. This busy traffic route between eastern and western Berlin achieved new fame in the techno era of the 90s with the **Love Parade**, brainchild of the self-styled Dr Motte. Every year this huge, carnival-like event attracts over a million ravers who come to drink, dance and celebrate to pounding techno rhythms. It is now a major economic factor, generating revenues of over Euro 125 million in just 24 hours. There is no doubt who has the best view of the show: "Golden Elsa" up on the 70m **Victory Column** overlooking the Hansa district and the new government buildings.

This strapping statue of Victoria weighs 37 tonnes, stands nearly nine metres tall and has shoe size 92. The monument with its gilded cannons commemorates Prussian victories between 1864 and 1871. The ascent is exhausting, but the panoramic view from the platform is well worth it.

Victory Volumn – Love Parade ▽

TRAIN STATIONS IN BERLIN

One of the capital's most ambitious new construction projects has been completed in time for the Soccer World Cup 2006: the new main station **Hauptbahnhof** – Europe's largest crossing station and therefore an architectural and engineering pièce de résistance. Above-ground, trains run in an east-west direction while train service is bundled in a north-south direction underground. Neighboring the Chancellery and Reichstag building, the first central main station in the history of Berlin is an important hub. From here, trains run in all directions at 90-second intervals. Each day, the futuristic building with its 320 m long glass track hall is frequented by approximately 300,000 passengers and visitors. In addition to the new main station, numerous other train stations also handle the long- and short-distance traffic: Gesundbrunnen, Südkreuz, **Spandau**, **Ostbahnhof**, **Wannsee** and **Lichtenberg**. Moreover, regional train connections also have the S-Bahn stations Friedrichstraße, **Alexanderplatz**, Lichterfelde Ost, Jungfernheide, **Potsdamer Platz**, and – West Berlin's former long-distance train station – **Zoologischer Garten**.

▽ Main station "Hauptbahnhof"

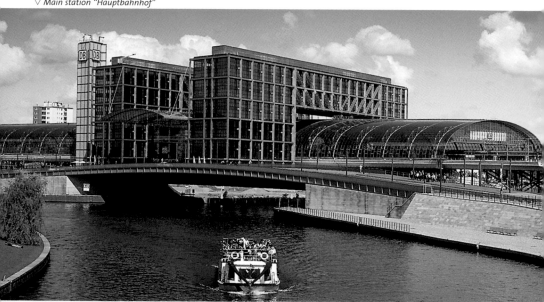

▽ Schlesisches Tor underground station

Hackescher Markt S-Bahn (urban rail) station ▽

THE REICHSTAG
Mitte, Platz der Republik

The design chosen for the original Reichstag parliament building was submitted by Paul Wallot, a virtually unknown architect from Frankfurt. Wallot's plans were changed repeatedly, however, most often by Kaiser Wilhelm II in person. As a result of these delays, it wasn't until 1894 that the building on what was then the Königsplatz finally went into service as the seat of the freely-elected government of the German people. The inscription over the main entrance, Dem Deutschen Volke ("To the German People"), was the subject of acrimonious debate for years. Following the Reichstag fire of 28 February 1933, which still remains a mystery, and further severe damage by the Red Army in April 1945, it was nearly half a century before the building once again became the home of Germany's parliament: In 1991, the MPs in Bonn voted by a narrow margin to move the Bundestag back to the Reichstag. During the years of West Berlin's isolation the building was restored, but the treaty between the four Allies forbade its use as a seat of government. Instead, it served as the venue for the permanent exhibition, Questions of German History. Strangely, the first time the building again attracted worldwide attention was in the summer of 1995 when the artist Christo wrapped it in shimmering silvery material for a week. Four million people came to enjoy the unusual spectacle. The subsequent complete renovation (45,000 tons of rubble were removed, only the shell remained intact) was performed with great sensitivity by top British architect Sir Norman Foster. One of the most striking features is the new glass cupola atop the building, with an ingenious system of mirrors that transports light down into the parliament chamber. The cupola's visitors' gallery makes it a popular tourist attraction. Every day, thousands of people queue patiently for hours to enjoy the panoramic view of Berlin's new buildings and watch the nation's parliament in action from above. Breakfast in the elegant roof garden bistro is regarded as particularly chic.

Reichstag building ▽

△ Federal Chancellery

▽ Reichstag building, the light well in the glass cupola

▽△ *Reichstag building*　　　　△ *Glass cupola*　　　　▽ *Parliament chamber*

PARLIAMENT BUILDINGS · EMBASSIES

On 26 June 1991, after a marathon 12-hour debate, the Bundestag decided by the slimmest of majorities (337 to 330) to move to Berlin, triggering an unprecedented flurry of fevered building activity in the city centre. Europe had never seen anything like it. It was around eight years before the Bonn MPs were able to convene for the first official session of parliament in "faraway" Berlin, on 19 April 1999. This was followed shortly afterwards by yet another important parliamentary procedure, the election of a new German president – former prime minister of North Rhine-Westphalia Johan-

nes Rau, one of the vehement supporters of Bonn as the permanent location for the German parliament. Be that as it may, the state's new number one immediately took up his duties and filled his official residence Schloss Bellevue with life and the ceremonial of protocol, following capably in the footsteps of his predecessors Herzog and von Weizsäcker, who had been a pioneer in favour of Berlin. **Schloss Bellevue**, built in 1785 and severely damaged in World War II, has remained peaceful and unchanged. Only the new administrative complex, the **German President's Office "Presidential Egg"**, reflects the necessities of gov

▽ *Ministry of the Interior*

▽ *Schloss Bellevue (Bellevue Palace)*

ernment in the new "Berlin Republic". This striking oval building was also the first to be undertaken in the new government quarter. Most of the projects, even those that seemed like audacious fantasies, have now been completed and are in service. The Federal Government alone brought 38 kilometres of files and 120,000 items of office furniture. Nearly all the players on the political stage now have new roofs over their heads. The SPD (Social Democrats) moved into their new headquarters before the CDU (Christian Democrats). Glass, symbol of transparency, is the dominant material in both buildings. The same applies to the new **Ministry of the Interios**, the **Federal Chancellery**, the **Federal Press Bureau** and the extension to the **Foreign Office**. The former Reich Aviation Ministry on the Wilhelmstrasse, designed by Ernst Sagebiel (who also built Tempelhof Airport), still the biggest office building in Berlin, is now the home of the **Federal Ministry of Finance**. Its 2,000 rooms have been completely modernised and renovated, just like the complexes housing the ministries of justice, economic affairs and transport. The **Bundesrat** (Federal Council, second legislative chamber of the German Government) occupies the former Preussisches Herrenhaus, a beautiful palace

Jungfernbrücke (Berlin's last drawbridge, with the Foreign Office in the background ▽

on the Wilhelmstrasse regarded by many experts as a consummately successful symbiosis of Wilhelmenian architecture and the third millennium. The embassies have also moved to Berlin Mitte, almost without exception; but in contrast to the Government, their buildings are almost all modern. Architectural visions of tomorrow are provided by the embassies of the five **Nordic states**, the neighbouring **Mexicans**, the **Austrians** and the **British**, who are once again right next door to Hotel Adlon. **Italy**, **Japan**, **Hungary**, **Switzerland**, **Russia** and **Spain** have all chosen to use their old embassy buildings, but they have all been thoroughly renovated. **France's** diplomats now reside in a brand-new, somewhat futuristic structure in the traditional location on Pariser Platz. The embassy of the **USA** on the other side of the square is a subject of ongoing debate and dispute. Among the capital's more striking new buildings are the "News Palace" of the **Federal Press Conference** with its fascinating lighting effects in the façade windows, the **Central ARD Studio** used jointly by the SFB and WDR broadcasting corporations, and the **"Moabit Snake"** on the Spree riverbank, which provides elegant and inexpensive accommodation for leading parliamentarians.

▽ *Federal Press Conference*

▽ *Russian embassy*

△ The Quadriga on Brandenburg Gate

Adlon Hotel, Pariser Platz ▽

BRANDENBURG GATE
Mitte, Pariser Platz

This gate is a national symbol and without doubt the country's most important secular building – it has been chosen as the motif for the reverse side of all German euro coins. Brandenburg Gate is the capital's only remaining intact city gate (at the time of Napoleon Berlin was guarded by 13 gates), and it is very much more than just a decorative entranceway to the splendid Unter den Linden boulevard. The Classicist ensemble, modelled on the Propylaeum on the Acropolis in Athens, was designed by Carl G. Langhans and completed in 1791. Strictly speaking, the Roman-style Quadriga atop the Greek Doric columns of the gateway is a jarring clash of styles. Despite this, however, the triumphant Goddess Victoria and her four stallions drawing her chariot homewards became world famous. The present lady and her horses are post-war reconstructions. All that is left of the originals, which were designed by Johann Schadow and executed by coppersmith Friedrich Jury, is a single horse's head, now safely stowed away in a museum. Everything else was either destroyed in May 1945 or appropriated and melted down.

▽ Brandenburg Gate

UNTER DEN LINDEN AVENUE

Mitte

The old royal Berlin of Prussia's heyday begins at **Pariser Platz**, Germany's most expensive address (where a piece of land the size of a beer mat would now cost over 125 euros). On 16 April 1647 the Great Elector decreed that trees should be planted along the boulevard leading to the Stadtschloss (City Palace, demolished in 1950). Gardener Michael Hanff created a shady avenue of linden and walnut trees, one thousand of each, between Brandenburg Gate and the palace. Its official name was the Gallerie, but the walnuts wilted and the lindens flourished and soon the Berliners all referred to it as Unter den Linden (Beneath the Lindens). The first post box was installed in 1824. Following the establishment of the German Reich in 1871 the Baroque villas were gradually replaced by modern office buildings, banks and hotels – including the **Adlon**, opened in 1907 and then reopened in 1997. The Dressler and Hiller restaurants were particularly famous. Today, Unter den Linden is dominated by cars and restaurants. The inner courtyard of the **Staatsbibliothek** (State Library) is a pleasant green oasis.

FRIEDRICH THE GREAT MONUMENT
Mitte, Unter den Linden

The statue of Friedrich II of Prussia has now returned to its time-honoured place. From his vantage-point 14 metres up, "Old Fritz" once again keeps watch over the goings-on Unter den Linden avenue. Christian D. Rauch's monument shows the monarch wearing his tricorn hat and mounted on his favourite steed, Condé. The masterminds of the GDR regime considered having the statue melted down, but even they balked at this and instead erected it in the wrong place in front of the university.

▽ *Friedrich the Great monument*

HUMBOLDT UNIVERSITY
Mitte, Unter den Linden 6

Friedrich the Great had the district west of the palace renovated and turned into the harmonious Forum Fridericianum. One of the new structures was an addition to the Zeughaus complex, built as a palace for his brother Prince Heinrich (1726–1802). It was designed by Dutch architect J. Boumann the Elder, who integrated it perfectly in the plan that G. W. von Knobelsdorff had drawn up for the king. Construction started in 1748 but the project wasn't completed until 1766. It was then the second largest building in

the city after the City Palace (Stadtschloss). After the prince's death it fell into disrepair. It then became the home of the new Berlin University in 1810, and the first deacons, Fichte, Hufeland, Schleiermacher and Biener, started teaching on 6 October. Six students were matriculated in the first year. This is where Max Planck worked out the foundations of the quantum theory that revolutionised modern physics, in the summer of 1900. Heine, Marx, Engels and Liebknecht all studied here, and the university's lecturers have included Humboldt, Virchow, Koch, Hahn, Sauerbruch and Einstein.

OLD LIBRARY – "KOMMODE"
Mitte, Unter den Linden/Bebelplatz

The Royal Library was built to complement the Unter den Linden State Opera House, drawing on the architectural ideals of Fischer von Erlach, who designed the Hofburg Theatre in Vienna. The Berliners immediately referred to it disrespectfully as the "Kommode" (chest of drawers). Hegel, Schopenhauer, the Grimm brothers, Ranke, Mommsen and Lenin all pored over heavy tomes here. An impressively modest monument commemorates the notorious Nazi book-burning that took place in front of the building on 10 May 1933.

▽ *Staatsbibliothek (State Library)*

Humboldt University ▽

Old Library – "Kommode" ▽

KRONPRINZENPALAIS
Mitte, Unter den Linden 3

Despite damage suffered in the last days of the war, the Crown Prince's Palace is still a striking landmark at the end of Unter den Linden avenue. The GDR regime restored the building and installed opulent quarters for guests of state, including West German politician Egon Bahr, who stayed here during the transit agreement negotiations in 1973. The reunification treaty between the GDR and West Germany was signed here in 1990. Today the building houses a branch of the German History Museum.

▽ *Kronprinzenpalais*

PRINZESSINNEN-PALAIS
Mitte, Unter den Linden

At the age of 13 the daughters of the kings of Prussia were separated from their brothers and moved to the Princesses' Palace for an upbringing as God-fearing, meek and chaste young ladies. An arch connects the palace with the Kronprinzenpalais. Like so many other buildings, the Prinzessinnen-Palais was reduced virtually to rubble in the wartime bombing. Following its restoration in the 60s it housed a patisserie. Today it is a popular café and restaurant where strollers stop in the garden for a gossip in good weather.

▽ *Prinzessinnen-Palais (Opernpalais)*

NEW GUARDHOUSE
Mitte, Unter den Linden 4

The last prisoner at the Neue Wache was the mayor of Köpenick, who was made immortal on 16 October 1906 by his involvement in the cobbler Wilhelm Vogt's masquerade as an army captain. The interior of Schinkel's original building (1816–1818) has been remodelled several times. Kollwitz' sculpture of the grieving mother, installed in the face of considerable opposition during Helmut Kohl's term of office as chancellor, is an urgent reminder of the horrors of war.

ST HEDWIG'S CATHEDRAL
Mitte, Bebelplatz

Friedrich the Great commissioned Knobelsdorff to design a Catholic cathedral, which was then completed by J. Boumann the Elder. It was built between 1747 and 1773 and gutted by fire in 1943. At heart, King Friedrich was really an atheist, but he was also great believer in tolerant coexistence, and after conquering Silesia he wanted to provide his new Catholic subjects with a fitting place of worship in Protestant Berlin. Today, St Hedwig's Cathedral is a cardinal's church.

▽ *New Guardhouse*

▽ *St Hedwig's Cathedral*

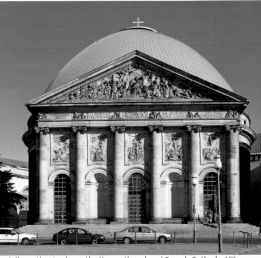

Gendarmenmarkt, Schauspielhaus theatre (now the Konzerthaus) and French Cathedral ▽

GENDARMENMARKT
Mitte

Many now once again claim that this is Europe's most beautiful square. Following completion of the new buildings around the perimeter, the classic ensemble of Schinkel's **Schauspielhaus** theatre (now the **Konzerthaus**) with its magnificent open-air staircase, flanked by the German and French cathedrals on the left and right, lends the Gendarmenmarkt an almost homey atmosphere. The many new bistros are popular haunts for trendy people intent on "seeing and being seen".

GERMAN AND FRENCH CATHEDRALS
Mitte, Gendarmenmarkt

Neither of these little churches with the identical spires are actually cathedrals. They got their names from the French word for cupola, dôme, which sounds like the German word for cathedral (Dom). The buildings now house two interesting exhibitions: **Questions of German History** (German Cathedral) and the **Huguenot Museum** (French Cathedral). The white **Schiller Monument** was hidden away in a storehouse for years before finding a new home here.

▽ *German and French Cathedral*

FRIEDRICHSTRASSE

Mitte

This avenue was planned by Friedrich I, the first King of Prussia, as a connection to Unter den Linden. It was also His Majesty who decreed that the precisely-aligned North-South axis should bear his name. The construction of the railway made this one of the busiest districts in Berlin. The **Friedrichstrasse railway station** (opened 1882, with a private waiting-room for the Kaiser) became the focal point of immoral activity during the long nights. For some years the Wintergarten, venue of the world's first public cinema screening, was Germany's biggest entertainment hall. Now that the torpor enforced by the city's division has ended, Friedrichstrasse is once again a lively and elegant connection between the new districts of Berlin Mitte and Kreuzberg-Friedrichshain. The three new connected blocks in the section to the west of the Gendarmenmarkt were conceived as direct competition to the Kurfürstendamm – they house some of the city's finest shops, including designer boutiques, **Quartier 206** and the elegant **Galéries Lafayette** department store.

▽ *The Galéries Lafayette department store*

"Writer's Block", corner of Friedrichstrasse/Schützenstrasse △

△ Französische Strasse underground station, Grand Hotel   ▽ Quartier 206 (inside)   △ Quartier 206   ▽ Stadtmitte underground station

CHECKPOINT CHARLIE
Friedrichshain-Kreuzberg, Friedrichstrasse 43–44

Today, little remains of this focal point of the Cold War – just a reconstructed Allied Nissen hut and a large mounted photograph in the middle of the road. This was once the control point for entry to East Berlin, where the conflicts between East and West were often at their most visible and dramatic. One of the most legendary and terrifying incidents took place in November 1961, when the tanks of the American and Red Armies stood face to face on either side of the white demarcation line, engines running and cannons loaded.

HAUS AM CHECKPOINT CHARLIE
Friedrichshain-Kreuzberg, Friedrichstrasse 44

When it came to escaping the yoke of communism, no plan was too fantastic, no escape route too daring. Despite the extreme danger, many of the people of the GDR were astoundingly creative in their attempts to cross the border into freedom. The exhibits at this unique museum include many of the curious utensils and items of equipment used in the escapes, most of which were successful. In addition to this the exhibition also provides extensive background information on the bitter underlying conflicts.

Checkpoint Charlie ▽

▽ *Sculpture on Bethlehemkirchplatz*

Mauermuseum · Checkpoint Charlie (Berlin Wall Museum) ▽

THE BERLIN WALL
East Side Gallery, *Mühlenstrasse*

It was built in the night of 12-13 August 1961. Not a single secret service had heard so much as a whisper about the meticulously-planned preparations. In time, the original primitive barricade of cinder blocks and barbed wire was replaced by a high, massive wall made of tuff stone with concrete reinforcement. Thus began the story of the Berlin Wall, which divided the city for 28 years, an infamous border at which many people were gunned down. The GDR regime referred to the horrific structure innocuously as the "antifascist barricade", perfecting the perfidy with gun emplacements, mines, watchtowers and electrified fences. In West Berlin lookout towers were built for coaches to stop and let the tourists gawp, postcard kiosks did a flourishing trade and artists covered the wall with graffiti. On the eastern side a lethal system of controls was set up that made attempts to climb across something that one could pay for with one's life. Today, there are just a few fragments left of the 40-kilometre Berlin Wall, for example at the **East Side Gallery**.

▽ *East Side Gallery*

▽ *East Side Gallery*

Breaching the wall in 1989 △

TEST THE BEST

POLITIK IST DIE FORTSETZUNG DES KRIEGES MIT ANDEREN MITTELN.

Memorial wall, Bernauer Strasse △▽

POTSDAMER PLATZ
Mitte

Over 150 years ago Berlin's very first railway station was built here. The first service was to Potsdam, and this gave both the station and (later) the square their names. Potsdam station had to be enlarged several times, and in the 20s Potsdamer Platz and the neighbouring Leipziger Platz became one of the busiest intersections in all Europe. This is where the Haus Vaterland (Fatherland House) once stood, and there were also countless dance halls, beer bars and wine pubs. The district was so popular that no fewer than 31 tram and bus lines converged here from all points of the compass. The crossroads was regulated by the very first traffic light system outside the USA. A copy of the first traffic light still stands in the original position. Since both the Reich Chancellery and Hitler's bunker were in the direct vicinity the entire district was bombed to the ground towards the end of the war. For nearly five decades after that it remained a deserted wasteland. Nobody could have predicted that just ten years after German reunification it would be one of the world's busiest

▽ *Potsdamer Platz with Sony Center*

building sites, consuming around 2.5 million euros in excavation costs every single day. To date, the entire Potsdamer Platz project has consumed over 5 billion euros, not including the railway investments. The **Debis Complex**, which includes the **Hyatt Hotel**, was followed by Berlin's new **Casino** and the **Sony Center**, a futuristic glass-fronted complex where the Deutsche Bahn AG (German Rail) also has its headquarters. The coveted Gold and Silver Bear awards are presented here at the Berlin Film Festival. The elegant, three-storey mall in the complex is now one of the busiest and highest-revenue shopping centres in Europe. When everything is finished, it is expected that the Potsdamer Platz station will be frequented by around a million people every day. This figure is absolutely realistic; the shops here are already open round the clock and the place pulses with life until far into the night. A relic of the past: the traditional **Huth wine shop and restaurant**. Also worth seeing: The remains of the old Hotel Esplanade, including the Kaisersaal lounge and the cocktail bar with its fine plasterwork and stucco decorations.

△ Beisheim-Center, Potsdamer Platz

▽ Marlene-Dietrich-Platz, Daimler Complex

△ Sony Center (inside)

The Potsdam Square Arcades shopping mall ▽

SCHLOSSBRÜCKE

Mitte, Karl-Liebknecht-Strasse

This splendid bridge was designed by Schinkel in 1822 to replace the plain and rather unpopular original structure that was referred to disparagingly as the "Dog Bridge". It spans the broad moat that separated the monarch from his subjects. The group of eight goddesses carrying the fallen young warriors to Olympus, carved out of white Carrera marble, commemorates the Wars of Liberation against Napoleon. The statues spent years in a warehouse in West Germany but were generously returned on the occasion of the 750th anniversary celebrations.

▽ *Schlossbrücke and Berlin Cathedral*

Berlin Cathedral　　　△ *Entrance*　　　*Main altar* ▷

BERLIN CATHEDRAL
Mitte, Am Lustgarten

Originally, a Classicist church designed by C. F. Schinkel stood on this site to the east of the Lustgarten park, which started life as the kitchen and herb garden of the Electoral Palace. Although the lovely structure was harmoniously integrated in its surroundings, Kaiser Wilhelm II was obsessed with the idea of turning Berlin into a city of art surpassing Paris and Rome. The old church didn't have any place in his plans and he had it demolished, replacing it with Berlin Cathedral, which he referred to as "Protestant Prussia's reply to Catholic Rome". Its architecture, subject of some controversy, combines both Baroque and Renaissance elements. Started by J. C. Raschdorff in 1894 and completed in 1905. The court church had room for a congregation of over 2,000 – for example at the traditional New Year's services attended by the Kaiser and his family. Despite severe damage in the War the ruin was not demolished. Now the crypt is open to the public again and the restoration of the interior, including the lovely mosaics, is almost complete. Excellent acoustics for concerts and oratorios.

◁ *The cathedral organ*

Berlin Cathedral ▽

MUSEUM ISLAND

Altes Museum · Neues Museum
Alte Nationalgalerie
Bode Museum · Pergamonmuseum
Between the Spree and the Kupfergraben

Included on the prestigious UNESCO World Cultural Heritage list, the Museum Island behind the Lustgarten houses a wealth of unique treasures. If you want to see everything you should schedule several full days for the project. The buildings were severely damaged during the War and some of the collections were also plundered by the Allied troops. Thanks to generous guaranteed federal subsidies, the **Prussian Cultural Heritage Foundation** that administers the island has been able to reconstruct and restore the buildings and recover many of their treasures. The situation was further complicated by the division of the city in 1948 and the building of the Berlin Wall in 1961, with all parties involved making claims that could not be satisfied. After German reunification full use was made of the unique opportunity for a fresh start. The collections have a broad span, extending from the roots of antiquity to the 19th century.

▽ *Pergamonmuseum, Pergamon altar*

▽ *Bode Museum*

The project was started by King Friedrich Wilhelm III and his son Friedrich Wilhelm IV, who was a great connoisseur of the arts. Both men believed firmly that they were the first servants of the state, and not just absolute monarchs who could rule as they saw fit. After the end of the Wars of Liberation and the overthrow of Napoleon they decided to turn the German capital into a place of beauty and introduce the newly-educated middle classes to the pleasures of the Greek and Roman classics. In 1824 the marshes between the Spree and Kupfergraben were filled and work began on the main structure, the **Altes Museum** (Old Museum). The design with its eighteen Ionic columns is by Schinkel. The 80-ton granite sculpture by C. C. Cantian in front of the building was installed in 1829. This "district dedicated to art and classical studies" is Berlin's oldest museum complex and the third-oldest in Germany. Other buildings include the **Neues Museum** (New Museum, completed in 1855) and the **Alte Nationalgalerie** (Old National Gallery, 1875). These were followed under the reign of Wilhelm II by the Kaiser Friedrich Museum, which is now called the **Bode Museum**,

Pergamonmuseum ▽

and the **Pergamonmuseum**, which was started in 1909 by A. Messel, whose designs echo the Doric elements used in the Brandenburg Gate. Wilhelm Bode (born 1845), who was both the leading museum pioneer in the German Reich and head curator of all Prussian museums (since 1872), died before the project was finally finished in 1930. The stone Pergamum Altar, brought to Berlin from Asia Minor in 1902 and widely regarded as one of the wonders of antiquity, is one of the greatest works of art in Europe. It was created in around 170 BC in honour of Zeus and Athena. After all the new building work has been completed in around 2008 the collections here will be restricted largely to exhibits from the pre-Christian period and the first two millennia of the Christian era. Most of the modern works will then be moved to Dahlem and the Kulturforum. This reorganisation of the collections will also mean that Berlin's most famous art treasure, the bust of Queen Nefertiti, will be moved to the Museum Island from its present home at the Egyptian Museum opposite Schloss Charlottenburg.

▽ *Altes Museum (Old Museum)*

▽ *Alte Nationalgalerie (Old National Gallery)*

MUSEUMS

Berlin has a confusing wealth of excellent, curious and surprising museums, spread out through all the capital's twelve districts. The quality and range of their collections makes the effort of tracking them down well worthwhile, however. The **Jewish Museum** is housed in the spectacular building on Lindenstrasse which was designed by D. Libeskind. A cultural centre in which "two thousand years of German-Jewish history" is kept alive with objects of art and everyday items. In addition to this permanent exhibition, the museum presents a wide range of readings, workshops and concerts and numerous temporary and special exhibitions exploring the Jewish culture which is rich in tradition. In the west wing of the Stüler building lovers of modern art can enjoy one of the most extensive collections of the works of Picasso and his contemporaries. Art collector Heinz Berggruen is the guiding spirit behind the **Berggruen Collection**. He agreed to sell the entire collection to the Berlin Council for the bargain price of just 100 million euros, payable in ten instalments. Behind the Stüler Building stands the **Bröhan Museum**, which specialises in commercial graphics and visual arts

Jewish Museum ▽

Museum für Gegenwart (Museum of the Present), in the former Hamburger railway station ▽

of the 20th and late 19th centuries, along with Art Nouveau, Art Deco and the Secession. The Eric Marx modern art collection at the **Museum für Gegenwart Berlin** (Museum of the Present) in the former Hamburger railway station also owes its existence to a private collector. The building in Dahlem that the **Gemäldegalerie** (Painting Gallery) moved into after the War was originally planned as an Asian Museum. In the future the main attractions in Dahlem building will be folk art from Europe and overseas and the **Geheime Staatsarchiv** (Secret State Archives). Also in Dahlem: the **Brücke-Museum** with paintings by Heckel, Nolde, Pechstein and others. The **Neue Nationalgalerie** on Potsdamer Strasse, designed by Mies van der Rohe, stages major exhibitions that receive worldwide coverage. Near Potsdamer Platz stands the **Kulturforum**, which houses the **Kunstgewerbemuseum** (Museum of Applied Art), the **Gemäldegalerie** (Painting Gallery), the **Kupferstichkabinett** (Collection of Prints and Drawings) and the **Kunstbibliothek** (Art Library). In the nearby Sony Complex is the **Film-museum** with a brand-new attraction: the entire personal estate of Marlene Dietrich. Technophiles shouldn't miss the **Deutsches Technikmuseum**,

▽ *Bust of Nofretete (circa 1350 BC)*

the **Luftwaffenmuseum** and the **Museum für Post und Telekommunikation**. If you're interested in history and politics try the **Deutsches Historisches Museum** in the **Zeughaus** (Berlin's most important Baroque building), the **Alliierten-Museum** (Allied Powers) and the **Museum Berlin-Karlshorst**. At the Allied Powers Museum in Dahlem a documentation of the months of the Berlin blockade and the airlift is on show in the Outpost, a cinema that was formerly only open to US military personnel. Exhibits in the grounds include an RAF transport plane from the airlift and a French officer's limousine. The building that houses the Museum Berlin-Karlshorst is the place where three Wehrmacht officers signed the unconditional capitulation to the four allied powers on 8 May 1945, marking the end of World War II in Europe. Also worth seeing: **Bauhausarchiv**, **Museum der Dinge** (Museum of Things), **Gedenkstätte Deutscher Widerstand** (German Resistance), **Topographie des Terrors** (Topography of Terror) and the **Feuerwehrmuseum** (fire brigade). Offbeat: **Zuckermuseum** (sugar), **Biermuseum** (beer), **Medizinhistorisches Museum** (medicalhistory), and of course Beate Uhse's **Erotikmuseum**.

Berggruen Collection ▽

Deutsches Historisches Museum in the Zeughaus ▽

THEATRES AND CONCERT HALLS

Around half a million people come to see the reviews at the **Friedrichstadtpalast** every year, and the **Deutsche Oper Berlin** attracts nearly 300,000 theatre-goers. Offering everything from scantily-clad dancing girls to epochal music from the orchestra pit, the capital's many theatres are very popular with locals and visitors alike. In all, nearly three million tickets are sold for the around ten thousand performances staged in the capital every twelve months. The political and media controversy over the cost of the arts subsidies (which now run into the billions) returns with the regularity of the seasons, but the net result for the city is definitely positive. Berlin's cultural and arts scene is unparalleled in Germany in terms of artistic variety, quantity and quality, and easily bears comparison with London and New York. Culture is an important factor in the economy of the city state. There are nearly fifty repertory theatres (including fifteen "public" establishments), four classical opera houses (plus the Neuköllner Oper as an experimental environment for talented newcomers), nine orchestras (which generally perform in the **Philharmonie**,

▽ *Theater des Westens*

the **Kammermusiksaal** and the **Konzerthaus** on the Gendarmenmarkt) and four professional choirs. And then there are a plethora of new cabaret and variety theatres, many of which are here today and gone tomorrow, a very lively off theatre scene, experimental theatre, comedy and much more besides - it wouldn't be possible to see everything even if you wanted to. Theatre, masquerade, satire and comedy have a long and venerable history in Berlin. The very first play, a pious epic, was performed here in 1541. The tradition of earthy entertainment for the masses was established by a Vien-

nese clown called Hans Schuch. Liberals and the educated circles enjoyed the charm of the French compagnies, whose popularity was often boosted by charming coquettes. But it was Friedrich the Great who brought "great art" to his subjects, among other things by building the **Staatsoper Unter den Linden** opera house in 1741–1743. His motto, FRIDERICVS REX APOLLINI ET MVSIS (King Friedrich for Apollo and the Muses), was inscribed over the six columns at the front of the building, and has been its guiding principle ever since. The **Komische Oper** in the Behrenstrasse (the previ-

▽ *Kammermusiksaal concert hall*

Philharmonie concert hall ▽

Maxim Gorki Theater ▽

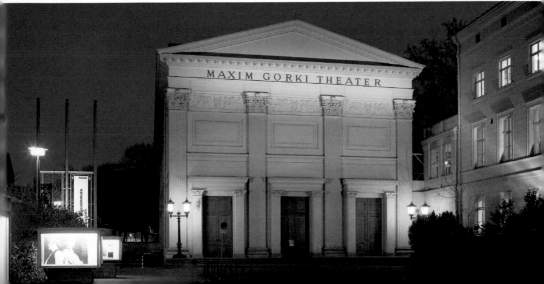

△ *Schauspielhaus (now the Konzerthaus) and French Cathedral*

Concert in the Schauspielhaus (now the Konzerthaus) ▽

ous building on the same site was the venue for the premieres of Lessing's first German comedy "Minna von Barnhelm" in 1767 and Goethe's "Goetz von Berlichingen" in 1774) and the **Deutsche Oper** in the Bismarckstrasse serve as inspirations, competition, examples and fellow travellers for the original Prussian opera house. Everyone in these opera companies - the musicians, soloists and all the other members of the teams – is committed to excellence in the service of the muses. This also applies without reservation to the **Berlin Philharmonic Orchestra**. Since its establishment in 1887, conductors like von Bülow, Nikisch, Furtwängler, von Karajan, Abado and Simon Rattle (who is takeing up the baton in the autumn of 2002) have made this one of the world's truly great classical orchestras. Today, Berlin's theatre scene is in full blossom, rivalling the golden era of the Twenties. The **Berliner Ensemble**, the **Deutsches Theater** and the associated **Kammerspiele**, the **Schaubühne on Lehniner Platz**, the **Volksbühne** on Rosa Luxemburg Platz, the **Maxim Gorki Theater**, the **Schlosspark Theater**, the **Renaissance Theater**, the **Tribüne** and the **Vaganten** perform both new interpretations

Staatsoper Unter den Linden ▽

of the classics and thought-provoking avant-garde productions. The **Komödie** and the **Theater am Kurfürstendamm** have already been Berlin's light entertainment Mecca for decades, with a repertoire ranging from witty comedies to earthy burlesque. The **Hebbel Theater** is committed to contemporary dance, while folksy farces are the speciality of the **Hansa Theater**. Intelligent cabaret is presented by the resident troupes at the **Stachelschweine** and the **Distel**, while the **Wühlmäuse** provides a new venue for visiting cabaret artists. The **Gripstheater** lures young theatre-goers and their more open-minded elders away from the pabulum of TV with bitingly critical contemporary works. Those who enjoy loud popular entertainment should try an evening at the **Musical Theater** on Potsdamer Platz or the **Theater des Westens**. The **Neuköllner Oper** a little outside the city centre is also well worth a visit – here one can experience the stars of tomorrow delivering masterly performances with the infectious verve and energy of youth and unforgettable voices. Finally, the **Theater zum westlichen Stadthirschen** is the city's top address for avant-garde theatre.

▽ *Friedrichstadtpalast*

▽ *Musical Theatre in "Daimler City" on Potsdamer Platz*

NEW SYNAGOGUE

Mitte, Oranienburger Strasse 30

The Neue Synagoge can hold a congregation of 3,200. Started in 1859 and completed by Friedrich A. Stüler, it was the city's main synagogue and religious centre for Berlin's entire Jewish community of around 160,000. The original building was gutted by fire in the infamous Kristallnacht of 9 November 1938, and the remaining shell was destroyed in an air raid in 1943. Since 1995 the golden Moorish cupola has been one of the main landmarks of the Scheunenviertel district. An exhibition documenting Jewish life can be seen in the foyer.

SCHEUNENVIERTEL

Mitte

Scheunenviertel means "Barn Quarter". The 1672 fire regulations forbade the storage of flammable materials like building materials, hay and straw within the city walls, and in the course of time 27 barns were built outside Oranienburg Gate. After 1720 the district also became densely populated and was known as Spandauer Vorstadt. It was a melting-pot and hotbed of poverty. Jews fleeing the pogroms in eastern Europe were one of the largest ethnic groups. They came seeking cheap accommodation, and gradually a Jewish ghetto grew up in the quarter.

New Synagogue ▽

HACKESCHE HÖFE · HACKESCHER MARKT

Mitte, Rosenthaler Strasse 40/41

Rosenthaler Strasse is in the district between Alexanderplatz square, Oranienburg Gate, Spandauer Vorstadt and the predominantly Jewish Scheunenviertel (Barn Quarter), a strategic location that already made it a busy centre of business 125 years ago. The district around the old Börse station (now Hackescher Markt) was one of the first planned communities, based on the ideas of Viennese city planner and sociologist Dr Martin A. Hetzenauer, who believed in integrating work, accommodation and leisure facilities. Premises for small shops and businesses, pubs and affordable homes were built around several large, bright back yards (Höfe). The Hackesche Höfe were the largest sites and the houses built here were the highest, with up to seven floors. They were not hit in the air raids and much of the original structures has survived intact. The renovation project carried out after reunification was a great success, creating a new culture, design and activity centre with cinemas and a cabaret theatre.

▽ *Hackescher Markt · Hackesche Höfe*

▽ *Hackesche Höfe*

NIKOLAIVIERTEL
Ephraim Palais · Nikolai Church
Mitte

The Nikolai quarter lives from its variety. The **Ephraim Palace** (Lessing lived here from 1752–1755) and the nearly 1,000-year-old **Nikolai Church** are surrounded by an identikit residential district out of the concrete mixer with numerous pubs, including the "Gerichtslaube", "Zur Rippe", "Paddenwirt", the prosperous Knoblauch family's early Classicist Bürgerhaus and the rebuilt "Nussbaum" (classic caricaturist and artist Heinrich Zille used to drink and draw in the original Nussbaum on Fischer Island). The district was planned and built by East Berlin's city council and completed on time for the 750th anniversary celebrations in 1987. It had urban flair and the 800 flats were sought-after (GDR secret service director Markus Wolf lived here). After reunification the shops here had some rough years. People still come here for a drink and a bit of sunshine on Sundays because it's centrally located and accessible without a car. The Knoblauch house is now the home of a rather twee local history museum and a romantic wine bar that serves food by candlelight.

Nikolaiviertel (Nikolai quarter) ▽

ALEXANDERPLATZ
Mitte

This square is a Berlin institution. Huge, loud, disproportional, loved and hated. It was immortalised as the stamping ground of antihero Franz Biberkopf in a book by Alfred Döblin, a doctor who served the poor. The "Alex" was originally a cattle market just outside the city limits. It got its name from the visit of Tsar Alexander. In 1930 it became an important traffic hub, with underground and urban rail lines on five levels. The Alexander and Berolina Bauhaus buildings are still worth seeing, even though they are a bit run down (designed by P. Behrens, Germany's leading industrial architect). Also interesting: the huge fresco on the former Haus des Lehrers (Teachers Building) by Walter Womacka, inspired by Mexican artist Diego Rivera. The fountain next to the restored World Time Clock is referred to colloquially as the "whore's brooch" (Nuttenbrosche) and was already a meetingplace for nonconformists and rebels under the GDR regime.

▽ *Red Town Hall*

RED TOWN HALL

Mitte, Rathausstrasse/Spandauer Strasse

The Rotes Rathaus is now the official seat of the governing mayor of united Berlin, who moved in after the general exodus from the world-famous Schöneberg Town Hall on October 3 1991. The red bricks used to build it came from a little village in the Mark near Berlin called Wassersuppe (Water Soup). Designed by Hermann F. Waesemann and built in 1859, the Rotes Rathaus is a hundred metres square and a hundred metres high (including the flagpole atop the tower). Open to the public.

MARIENKIRCHE (CHURCH OF OUR LADY)

Mitte, Karl-Liebknecht-Strasse 8

First mentioned in 1294, the original Marienkirche was a plain nave church made of rough stone. It was the centre of the New Town that grew up by the ford between Cölln and Berlin. After several fires it was rebuilt in 1420 and two side aisles were added. Bach once played on the church's silver organ. The Dance of Death frieze in the vestibule of the north bell tower is one of Berlin's oldest art treasures, started in 1485. It is two metres high and 22 metres long.

Alexanderplatz (Alexander Square) ▽

Marienkirche (Church of Our Lady) ▽

OLYMPIC STADIUM

Charlottenburg-Wilmersdorf, Olympischer Platz

The Olympic stadium on the Reichssportfeld was originally built for the summer games in 1936. It is now a little run down and is going to be fully renovated, at a cost of nearly a quarter of a billion euros, to prepare it for the world cup final in 2006. The complex is the largest sports facility in Europe and includes the Maifeld, sports halls, hockey fields, the swimming stadium, the Waldbühne outdoor stage (used for rock and classical concerts) and the bell tower with one of the city's finest panoramic views (with an elevator).

FUNKTURM (BROADCASTING TOWER)

Charlottenburg-Wilmersdorf, Messedamm 11

The Funkturm is one of the city's most prominently visible landmarks, also at night, when it is floodlit. Much loved by homecoming Berliners, who always breathe a sigh of relief when they see it rearing up over the **AVUS ring**. The 150-metre structural steel framework was built in 1925 by H. Straumer for the third Berlin broadcasting fair. The first experimental television broadcasts were transmitted from here in 1931. The restaurant with its exquisite wooden panelling has aged gracefully and is still very much worth a visit.

▽ *Olympic Stadium*

▽ *Olympic Stadium, inside*

ICC and Exhibition Centre
Charlottenburg-Wilmersdorf

The original Kongresshalle in the Tiergarten district soon proved to be too small. Between 1973 and 1979 it was replaced by the ICC, which was then the most expensive and futuristic structure in all West Berlin. Originally highly controversial, it is still the city's most massive building, 320 metres long, 80 metres wide and with a volume of 800,000 cubic metres. Even though it can handle congresses with 20,000 participants it is now once again too small for many events, and possible extensions are being discussed.

House of World Cultures
Mitte, John-Foster-Dulles-Allee

The Haus der Kulturen der Welt, donated by the USA, was originally built as a congress hall for the Interbau construction fair in 1957. It was designed by H. Stubbins, one of the pioneers of avant-garde concrete architecture. In 1980 it turned out that the structure of the popular "pregnant oyster" was faulty: the roof collapsed. It was reopened in 1987 as a forum for artists from the Third World and developing countries. The huge Henry Moore sculpture next to the outside staircase is one of the most important modern art works in Berlin.

ICC and Exhibition Centre · Funkturm (Broadcasting Tower) ▽

House of World Cultures (Haus der Kulturen der Welt, former Kongresshalle) ▽

ZOOLOGICAL GARDEN

Charlottenburg-Wilmersdorf, Hardenbergplatz 8

This was Germany's first zoo, created in 1844 when King Friedrich Wilhelm IV ordered that the collection of exotic animals that had previously lived on Peacock Island should be moved to the present location. Berlin Zoo in the city centre now has more species than any other in the world, with a total of nearly 16,000 animals. In 1955, following the division of the city, another zoo was opened by Schloss Friedrichsfelde – actually more of a wildlife park. The spacious enclosures give the impression that the 5,000 animals are living in the wild.

BOTANICAL GARDEN

Steglitz-Zehlendorf, Unter den Eichen 5–10

Berlin's first botanical garden was by the Berliner Schloss, where the Lustgarten stands to the west of the cathedral today. The second was established at the Kleistpark. The botanical garden in Dahlem with its huge palm house is the capital's third home for exotic flora. Some of the plants were grown from seeds brought to Berlin 250 years ago by Alexander von Humboldt. Today, workshops and exhibitions in the complex are popular with Berliners and visitors alike.

▽ *Zoological Garden, Elephant Gate*

▽ *Botanical Garden*

AIRPORTS

The plan is one of the city's perennial political issues: The old airport in **Tempelhof**, which is centrally located and not used to full capacity, is to be closed down. **Tegel** airport, overloaded and long since bursting at the seams, is a thorn in the side of the environmentalists. And **Schönefeld** airport is to be expanded and turned into a major facility serving all of Berlin and Brandenburg. When and how all these plans will be realised is another question altogether, however. Even the optimists don't believe the work can begin before 2009, and the pessimists put the date ten years later...

LAKES AND EXCURSIONS

"Nuthin' could be keener than a cruise on a steamer!" No matter whether young, old, poor or rich, the Berliners are fun-loving people who enjoy a day out on the water. Steam has now gone the way of the horse and carriage, of course, but you can still enjoy rides on vessels of all shapes and sizes on the **Havel** and **Spree** rivers and **Wannsee** and **Müggelsee** lakes. Sitting in the sun, feeding the gulls and quaffing a couple of beers are all essential parts of the Berlin lifestyle and something that every visitor should try.

Tegel airport ▽

Schönefeld airport ▽

PEACOCK ISLAND · LUSTSCHLOSS
Steglitz-Zehlendorf, Havel River

At the end of the 17th century the alchemist Johannes Kunckel from Rendsburg, scion of a Bohemian glass-maker's family, was summoned to the court of the Great Elector to make good his claim that he could turn base metal into gold. To ensure that the project remained secret his experimental laboratory was banished to the island of Kaninchenwerder in the Havel just outside Potsdam. Kunckel's attempts to produce gold failed, but in 1677 he accidentally discovered the recipe for making red glass, which was henceforth known as Kunckel glass. His laboratories then fell into disrepair. The next building on the island was the result of a liaison between King Friedrich Wilhelm II and Wilhelmine Encke. In 1795 the court carpenter Johann G. Brendel built a summer palace disguised as a ruin for the trysting couple, with an unrestricted view of Potsdam. The King's son, Friedrich Wilhelm III, spent the summer months there with his wife Luise and introduced the peacocks that gave the island its new name (German: Pfaueninsel). The Schloss and the (reconstructed) little dairy farm on the north shore are both open to visitors.

▽ Wannsee

▽ Peacock Island (Pfaueninsel), Lustschloss

Historical
Berlin

The Wall
1961–1989

West/East Berlin border
crossing points

1 Bornholmer Strasse
2 Chausseestrasse
3 Invalidenstrasse
4 Friedrichstrasse
  Checkpoint Charlie
5 Heinrich-Heine-Str.
6 Oberbaumbrücke
7 Sonnenallee

INFORMATION · ADDRESSES

▷ **BERLIN DIALING CODE**
+49-(0)30

▷ **TOURIST INFORMATION**
Tourist Info Center, Europa-Center
(entrance Budapester Strasse 45)
Mo-Sa 8:30-20:30h
Su 10:00-18:30h
Tourist Info Center,
Brandenburg Gate, south wing,
9:30-18:00h daily
Tourist Info Café, Broadcasting Tower,
Alexanderplatz, Panoramastrasse 1a
1.5.-30.9.: Mo-Sa 9-20h,
Su 10-18h
1.10.-30.4.: Daily 10-18h
Reservations line: +49 (0)30-250-025
Information: 0190-016-316
From abroad: +49-700-8623-7546
www.berlin-tourism.de

▷ **AIRPORTS, RAILWAYS & LOCAL TRANSPORT**
Tegel Airport
Tempelhof Airport
Schönefeld Airport
Central airport line: 01805-000-186
Deutsche Bahn AG (German Rail),
Tel: 297-0
Travel info: 194-19,
daily 06:00-23:00h
Travel info: 0180-599-6633 (24 hrs)
Berliner Verkehrsbetriebe (BVG, Local Transport Authority)
Tel: 194-49

▷ **SIGHTSEEING TOURS**
BVG Top Tour,
Tel: 2562-4740
BVB,
Tel: 885-9880
Tempelhofer Reisen, Tel: 572-4056
Severin & Kühn, Tel: 880-4190
Berolina Sightseeing,
Tel: 8856-8030, Fax: 8824-128
Stattreisen Berlin e.V., Tel: 4553-028

▷ **RENTALS**
Velo Taxi, rental rikshas
Saarbrücker Strasse 20-21,
Tel: 4435-8990 & 0172-3288-888
Nouri Rikscha OHG,
Wrangelstrasse 23,
Tel: 4023-685 & 0177-235-547

▷ **EMERGENCY SERVICES**
Fire/rescue service,
112
Police/emergencies,
110

▷ **BREAKDOWN SERVICES**
ACE-Autoclub Europa
Tel: 01802-343-536
ADAC Berlin-Brandenburg
Tel: 0180-222-2222

▷ **LOST PROPERTY OFFICES**
Central Office
Platz der Luftbrücke 6,
Tel: 6965

BVG Transport Authority Office
Fraunhofer Strasse 33-36
Tel: 2562-3040

▷ **TAXIS**
Tel: 210-101, 261-026, 690-22,
443-322, 0800-222-2255 free taxi
reservations

▷ **SIGHTS**
Berlin Cathedral (Berliner Dom)
Am Lustgarten,
Visitors service: 2026-9119
Concert tickets: 2026-9136
Daily 9-20h
Brandenburg Gate
Pariser Platz
German Cathedral (Deutscher Dom)
Am Gendarmenmarkt,
Tel: 2022-690 (Tu-Su 10-18h)
New Synagogue Berlin Centrum Judaicum
Oranienburger Strasse 28/30,
Tel: 2840-1250
Su-Th 10:00-17:30h,
Fr 10:00-13:30h
Broadcasting Tower
Panoramastrasse 1a, Tel: 2423-333,
Telecafe: 1 Mar-31 Oct 10-1h,
1 Nov-28 Feb 10-24h
Observation floor
1 Mar-31 Oct 9-1h,
1 Nov-28 Feb 10-24h
French Cathedral (Französischer Dom)
Gendarmenmarkt 5,
Tel: 2041-507, Tu-Sa 12-17h,
Su 11-17h, lookout gallery:
Daily 11-17h
Broadcasting Tower (Exhibition Centre)
Hammarskjöldplatz, Tel: 3038-0
Viewing platform: Daily 10-22h
Restaurant: Daily 11:30-23h
German Resistance Memorial,
Stauffenbergstr. 13/14,
Tel: 2699-5000,
Mo-We & Fri. 9-18h,
Sa, Su & holidays 10-18h
Plötzensee Memorial
Hüttigpfad, Tel: 3443-226
Mar-Oct 9-17h, Nov-Feb 9-16h
Wannsee Conference House –
Memorial and Educational Centre
Am Grossen Wannsee 56-58,
Tel: 805-001-0
Mo-Fr 10-18h, Sa & Su 14-18h
Neue Wache (New Guardhouse)
Unter den Linden 4
Nikolai Church (Nikolaikirche)
Nikolaikirchplatz
Tel: 2424-467, Tu-Su 10-18h,
last admission 17:30h

Palais am Festungsgraben
Am Festungsgraben 1,
Tel: 2384-145
Reichstag Building
Platz der Republik,
Tel: 2270, Cupola daily 8-22h
Roof garden restaurant:
Tel: 2262-990
Reservations: 2262-9933
Red Town Hall (Rotes Rathaus)
Rathausstr./Spandauer Str.,
Tel: 9026-0, Mo-Fr 9-18h
(except during events)
Schloss Glienicke
Königstrasse 36,
Tel: 8053-041, Sa & Su 10-17h
Victory Column (Siegessäule)
Grosser Stern/Strasse des 17 Juni,
Tel: 3912-961
Apr-Oct 9:30-18:30h,
Nov-Mar 9:30-17:30h
Church of Our Lady (Marienkirche)
Karl-Liebknecht-Strasse 8,
Tel: 2424-467, Mo-Th 10-16h,
Sa & Su 12-16h
Peacock Island Schloss and Gardens (Pfaueninsel)
Pfaueninselchaussee, Tel: 8053-042
May-Aug 8-20h daily,
and by appointment
Topography of Terror
Niederkirchner Str. 8,
Tel: 2548-6703
May-Sep 10-20h, Oct-Apr 10-18h,
and by appointment
Schloss Charlottenburg
Spandauer Damm, Tel: 32091-1
Tu-Fr 9-17h, Sa & Su 10-17h
Spandauer Zitadelle (Spandau Citadel)
Am Juliusturm, Tel: 3549-440
Tu-Fr 9-17h, Sa & Su 10-17h

▷ **MUSEUMS**
MDinfoline, Tel: 2839-7444
Museum Island (Museumsinsel)
Pergamonmuseum
Tel. 2090-5566
Tu-Su 10-18h, Th until 22h
Altes Museum
Tel. 2090-5244, Tu-Su 10-18h
Alte Nationalgalerie
Tel. 20 90 58 01
Tu-Su 10-18h, Th until 22h
Bode Museum (partially closed until 2006 for renovations)
Egyptian Museum (closed for the moment)
Bauhaus Archive
Klingelhöferstrasse 14,
Tel: 254-002-0, We-Mo 10-17h
Bröhan Museum
Schlossstrasse 1a,
Tel: 3269-0600, Tu-Su 10-18h

Brücke Museum
Bussardsteig 9,
Tel: 8312-029, We–Mo 11–17h
Deutsches Historisches Museum
Unter den Linden 2, Tel: 203-040
Deutsche Guggenheim Berlin
Unter den Linden 13–15,
Tel: 202-093-0, Daily 11–20h
Deutsches Technikmuseum Berlin
Trebbiner Str. 9, Tel: 254-840
Tu–Fr 9–17:30h, Sa & Su 10–18h
Ephraimpalais, Poststr. 16,
Tel: 240-020, Tu–Su 10–18h
Ethnologisches Museum (formerly Museum für Völkerkunde)
Lansstrasse, Tel: 2090-5555,
Tu–Fr 10–18h, Sa & Su 11–18h
Filmmuseum Berlin
Deutsche Kinemathek in the Sony
Center on Potsdamer Platz,
Tel: 30090-30, Fax: 30090-313
Tu–Su 10–18h, Th 10–20h
Friedrichswerdersche Church
(Schinkel Museum)
Werderscher Markt/Oberwallstrasse,
Tel: 208-1323, Tu–Su 10–18h
Galerie der Romantik
(In the east wing of Charlottenburg
Palace), Spandauer Damm,
Tel: 2090-5555
Tu–Fr 10–18h, Sa & Su 11–18h
**Gemäldegalerie
(Painting Gallery)**
Matthäikirchplatz, Kulturforum,
Tel: 266-2101
Tu–Su 10–18h, Th until 22h
Georg Kolbe Museum
Sensburger Allee 25,
Tel: 3042-144, Tu–Su 10–17h
Hamburger Bahnhof
Invalidenstr. 50–51,
Tel: 2090-5555, Tu–Fr 10–18h,
Sa & Su 11–18h, Th until 22h
Haus am Checkpoint Charlie
Friedrichstr. 44,
Tel: 253-725-0, Daily 9–22h
Jüdisches Museum
Lindenstr. 9–14
Tel. 2599-3300, Fax: 2599-3409
Tu–Su 10–20h, Th until 22h
Käthe Kollwitz Museum
Fasanenstr. 24,
Tel: 8825-210, We–Mo 11–18h
**Museum of Applied Art
(Kunstgewerbemuseum)**
Tiergartenstr., Kulturforum,
Tel: 2090-5555
Tu–Fr 10–18h, Sa & Su 11–18h
**Kupferstichkabinett
(prints & drawings)**
Matthäikirchplatz, Kulturforum,
Tel: 2090-5555
Tu–Fr 10–18h, Sa & Su 11–18h
Märkisches Museum
Am Köllnischen Park 5,

Tel: 308-660, Tu–Su 10–18h
Martin Gropius Building
Niederkirchner Str. 7,
Tel: 254-860, We–Mo 10–20h
**Museum für Naturkunde
(natural history)**
Invalidenstr. 43
Tel: 2093-8540, Tu–Su 9:30–17h
Neue Nationalgalerie
Potsdamer Str., Kulturforum,
Tel: 2662-651, Tu–Fr 10–18h,
Sa & Su 11–18h, Th until 22h
**Berggruen Collection
(Sammlung Berggruen)**
Schlossstrasse, Westlicher Stülerbau
(opposite Charlottenburg Palace)
Tel: 2090-5555, Tu–Fr 10–18h, Sa
& Su 11–18h
▷ **FLORA & FAUNA**
Aquarium, Budapester Str. 32,
Tel: 254-010, Daily 9–18h
Botanischer Garten
Königin-Luise-Str. 6–8,
Tel: 83006-0, Daily from 9h
Britzer Garten
Sangerhauser Weg 1, Tel: 700-906-0,
from 9h until nightfall
Tierpark Friedrichsfelde (zoo)
Am Tierpark 125,
Tel: 515-310, Daily 9–18h
Zoologischer Garten Berlin AG (zoo)
Hardenbergplatz 8/Budapester Str.
32, Tel: 254-010, Daily from 9h
▷ **CLASSICAL MUSIC
AND OPERA**
Deutsche Oper Berlin
Bismarckstr. 35
Komische Oper
Behrenstr. 55–57,
Konzerthaus Berlin
(in the Schauspielhaus am Gen-
darmenmarkt), Gendarmenmarkt 2
Neuköllner Oper
Karl-Marx-Str. 131–133,
Tel: 6889-0777
Philharmonie,
Herbert-von-Karajan-Str. 1,
Staatsoper Unter den Linden
Unter den Linden 7, Tel: 2035-4555
▷ **THEATRES**
bat-Studiotheater
Belforter Str. 15,
Tel: 4427-613
Berliner Ensemble
Bertold-Brecht-Platz 1,
Tel: 2823-160-284-081-55 & 50
Deutsches Theater/Kammerspiele
Schumannstr. 13a/14,
Grips Theater
Altonaer Strasse 45,
Hebbel Theater
Stresemannstr. 29,
Hansa-Theater
Alt-Moabit 48,
Tel: 3914-460

**Komödie & Theater am
Kurfürstendamm**
Kurfürstendamm 206 & 209,
Tel: 4799-7440
Maxim Gorki Theater
Am Festungsgraben 2,
Tel: 2022-1129 & 2022-1115
Renaissance Theater
Hardenbergstr. 6,
Schaubühne am Lehniner Platz
Kurfürstendamm 153, Tel: 890-023
Schlosspark-Theater
Schossstr. 48,
Theater im Palais
Am Festungsgraben 1,
Tel: 2010-693-95
**Theater zum
Westlichen Stadthirschen**
Kreuzbergstrasse 37,
Tel: 7857-033
Tribüne
Otto-Suhr-Allee 18,
Tel: 3412-600
Vaganten Bühne
Kantstr. 12a, Tel: 3124-529
Volksbühne
Rosa-Luxemburg-Platz,
Tel: 2476-772
▷ **MUSICALS, VARIETY,
CABARET**
Bar jeder Vernunft
Schaperstr. 24,
BKA, Mehringdamm 34,
Tel: 2510-112
Chamäleon Varieté
Rosenthaler Str. 40/41,
Tel: 2827-118 & 2385-769
Chez Nous
Marburger Str. 14, Tel: 2131-810
Estrel Festival Center
Sonnenallee 225,
Friedrichstadtpalast
Friedrichstr. 107
Grüner Salon
In der Volksbühne
Rosa-Luxemburg-Platz,
Tel: 2406-5807
Kabarett "Die Distel"
Friedrichstr. 101,
Kabarett "Die Stachelschweine"
Tauentzienstr. 9-12, Tel: 2614-795
La Vie en Rose
Tempelhof Airport, Tel: 6951-3000
Musical Theater Berlin
Marlene-Dietrich-Platz 1
Scheinbar-Varieté
Monumentenstr. 9, Tel: 7845-539
Theater des Westens
Kantstr. 12
Die Wühlmäuse am Theo
Pommerallee 1 (corner of Heerstr.)
Theater der Freien Volksbühne
Schaperstr. 24, Tel: 8842-0884
Wintergarten – Das Varieté
Potsdamer Str. 96

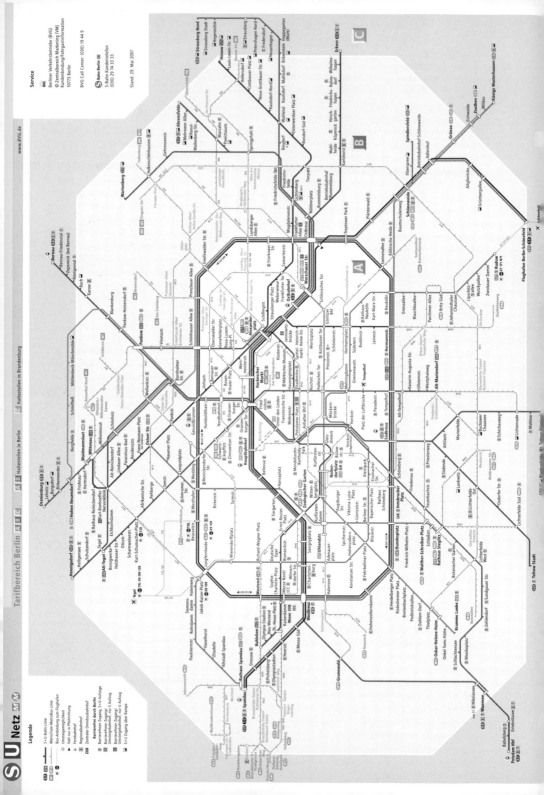

POTSDAM · SCHLOSS SANSSOUCI AND PARK

Schopenhauerstrasse/Zur historischen Mühle

Even in his youth King Friedrich II already started making plans to turn his back on Berlin and reside in a vigne, a kind of small wine-grower's cottage, near Potsdam. It is possible that these notions were inspired by the philosopher Voltaire. The monarch himself drew the first rough sketches and ordered his architect Georg W. von Knobelsdorff to use them as the basis for his plans. The name Sanssouci was an idea of von Knobelsdorff; in his youth he had often spent time in the house of the von Manteuffel family, whose estate was called "Kummerfrei". This was then freely translated to the French "Sans Souci" (without care). After a dispute between the royal client and his architect, von Knobelsdorff fell into disfavour and the palace, which looks wonderfully delicate despite its impressive size, was completed in 1748 by Johann Boumann from Holland. The terrace overlooking the artificial hillside vineyards remained the dominant feature of the palace hill. When it was finished, after the privations of the Seven Years' War,

▽ *Schloss Sanssouci (Sanssouci Palace) with terraces and the "Parterre", planted with Reseda vines*

Friedrich the Great lived there and surrounded himself with a circle of leading thinkers, statesmen, Enlightenment philosophers and even the Venetian rake Giacomo Casanova. The art-loving monarch was himself an outstanding flautist, the beloved greyhounds who had always accompanied him. "Women and parsons" were not welcome in the father of the nation's palace, however. Between 1763 and 1769 Friedrich II built the **New Palace** with 300 rooms in the Schloss Park at the end of the main avenue. His primary motive was to create qualified jobs and generate work for the building industry, which had been devastated by three Silesian wars. Friedrich's successors (including the art-loving italophile Friedrich Wilhelm IV) made major additions to the **Park** of Sanssouci, turning the 740-acre estate into one of the most beautiful palace and park complexes in all Europe. Friedrich II died here on 17 August 1786, and on 18 August 1991 his remains were finally buried here, as he had originally ordered in his will: beneath a plain stone slab and surrounded by his dogs.

△ Sanssouci, Orangery

▽ Schloss Sanssouci (Sanssouci Palace), Friedrich II's concert room

△ *Sanssouci, the New Palace (Neues Palais)*

▽ *Sanssouci, Chinese Tea House (1754–1757)*

POTSDAM · SCHLOSS CECILIENHOF
Am Neuen Garten

Crown Prince Wilhelm, son of Wilhelm II, had this modern mansion built on the shore of Heiligen See between 1914 and 1917. It was designed in the English country house style, with a two-storey hallway and even a recirculating air conditioning system! The revolution of 1918 forced him to flee briefly, but then he returned and lived in the half-timbered building with the famous Danzig Guild Staircase until 1944. In the summer of 1945 the three allied powers met here for the historic Potsdam Conference.

POTSDAM · BABELSBERG
Park Babelsberg

The palace complex in Babelsberg was built in the Tudor style considered modern at the time by Prussia's state architect Carl F. Schinkel, who "borrowed" liberally from the designs of Windsor Castle. The first wing near the Havel river was completed in 1835. Even in his old age the later Kaiser Wilhelm I continued to be very fond of the chilly and rather gloomy residence far from Berlin. Today, Babelsberg is mainly notable as a cinema city because of the modern media and studio centre on the former Ufa complex.

▽ *Schloss Cecilienhof (Cecilienhof Palace) in the New Garden*